S0-BRA-730

The Hindu Temple

Other books by Alain Daniélou

The Complete Kama Sutra (first unabridged modern translation)

Gods of Love and Ecstasy

Music and the Power of Sound

The Myths and Gods of India

The Phallus

Virtue, Success, Pleasure, and Liberation

While the Gods Play

Yoga: Mastering the Secrets of Matter and the Universe

The
Hindu Temple

Deification of Eroticism

Alain Daniélou

Translation by
Ken Hurry

Inner Traditions
Rochester, Vermont

Inner Traditions International
One Park Street
Rochester, Vermont 05767
www.InnerTraditions.com

First U.S. edition published by Inner Traditions in 2001
Originally published in French under the title *Le temple hindou
Centre magique du monde* in 1977
Published in Italian under the title *L'Erotismo divinizzato* by
Edizioni di red studio redazionale, 1999

Copyright © 1994, 1999 by Jacques Cloarec
English translation copyright © 2001 by Inner Traditions International

All rights reserved. No part of this book may be reproduced or utilized in any form or by any
means, electronic or mechanical, including photocopying, recording, or by any information
storage and retrieval system, without permission in writing from the publisher.

LIBRARY OF CONGRESS CATALOGING-IN-PUBLICATION DATA
Daniélou, Alain.
[Temple hindou, centre magique du monde. English]
The Hindu Temple : deification of eroticism / Alain Daniélou ; translation
by Ken Hurry.
p. cm.
Includes bibliographical references and index.
ISBN 0-89281-854-9 (alk. paper)
1. Temples, Hindu. 2. Erotica—Religious aspects—Hinduism. I. Title.

BL1243.74.D36 2000
294.5'35—dc21
00-047275

Printed and bound in the United States

10   9   8   7   6   5   4   3   2   1

Text design and layout by Virginia Scott-Bowman
This book was typeset in Sabon with Galliard as the display typeface

Contents

PART THREE

❦

Revealing the Divine Mind

❦

Introduction

Triggered by climatic changes that drove the peoples of central Asia toward India and Europe, the Aryan invasions that began at the outset of the second millennium B.C.E. profoundly changed the culture and religion of India, the Middle East, and Europe. Up to then, civilization had been largely uniform, stretching from India as far as Western Europe. This civilization is known to us only through archeological finds and the meager information surviving in myths, popular religion, and customs. The main religion of this culture, the source of all later civilizations, was Shaivism, which arose around 6000 B.C.E. with a tradition that has been uninterrupted only in India. The beliefs of this first great religion periodically reappear in popular tradition, since it is first and foremost a religion of the people.

Shaivism is characterized by worship of the principle of life, whose symbol is the phallus; by the cult and sacrifice of the bull, considered as the vehicle of Shiva, the male principle; by spring festivals to celebrate the world's rebirth; and by the techniques of Yoga, which aim to transform sexual potency into spiritual power.

Shaivite myths and rites form the substrate of all subsequent religions, as for example the Egyptian myths and cult of Osiris, the Dionysian and Bacchic legends and rites of Greece and Rome, the cult of the Minotaur in Crete, the Islamic Dhikr practices, or the carnivals and traditional bull races in Europe today. The fundamental aspects of this religion are worship of the phallus as the source of life, the reverence for the union of opposites in the sexual act as the image of the creative principle, and the divinization of erotic enjoyment as a reflection of divine bliss.

The *Puranas,* the ancient Hindu texts narrating the origins and principles of Shaivism, strongly emphasize the principle according to which whoever worships the phallus and honors the sexual life in all its forms will be favored by the gods. Whoever rejects or disdains them, on the other hand, will be struck down by divine wrath.

According to Shaivite prophecy, humanity's sole hope of survival resides in the current revolutionary struggle for sexual liberation. Only the worship of the principle of life and its symbol the phallus can draw down heaven's blessing on humankind, which is threatened by divine wrath at a civilization whose ethic, instead of happiness, joy, and pleasure, pursues war, sexual repression, hypocrisy, and the persecution of love. The Shaivite *Puranas* tell us that in the Kali Yuga (the era of conflicts in which we are now living), only the "fervent in love"—the adepts of the cult of Shiva-Dionysus who practice the bacchanalia—can save the world from destruction.

The seventh century C.E. saw the rebirth of Shaivism, which had survived the persecutions of Aryan Vedism (represented by the *brahman* caste) and of Buddhism (propounded by the military and princely caste of the *kshatriyas*).

From the seventh century to the arrival of the Muslims in the thirteenth century, a vast movement of popular faith—which can only be likened to what, in the western Middle Ages, gave rise to the building of the cathedrals—led to the construction of a surprising number of marvelous temples. The Muslims destroyed those located in the towns, but some of those built outside the Islamized areas—or in abandoned towns and cities, surrounded by forests or deserts—managed to survive.

The most beautiful medieval temples are located on a strip of land, only a few hundreds of kilometers wide, that crosses central India, starting from Orissa on the east coast, south of Bengal, to the desert of Rajputana on the western borders with Pakistan. In the whole of this vast area, which boasted thousands of temples, the only ones to survive vandalism are those located on abandoned sites in central India, now isolated in the forested interior of the Deccan. Others are lost in the deserts of Rajasthan and can only be reached by camel.

Today there are still about a hundred such sites where we can admire temples that have been fairly well preserved. Some sites have only one temple, whereas others contain several. Some of the most important buildings have fallen down, whereas others—although in theory protected as historic monuments—have been disfigured by the antique dealers of Bombay and Delhi, who have removed parts of the statues.

The most important sites are Bhuvaneshvar and Konarak in Orissa, and Khajuraho in central India. At Bhuvaneshvar and Khajuraho, more than ten temple groups, covered with wonderfully preserved sculptures, can be admired.

The ancient architectural treatises formally state that a temple lacking erotic representations is ineffective, maleficent, and will inevitably be struck by lightning. This means that besides the significance of the sculptures in the symbolic whole represented by the temple layout, sculptures are deemed to possess a direct magical capacity. Even in certain dwellings, erotic frescoes are deemed to keep the evil eye and bad luck at bay.

Today, few houses are permanently decorated with such frescoes, but for important ceremonies, particularly initiations and weddings, specialized artists use vivid colors to depict what are sometimes very suggestive love scenes on walls that have just been whitewashed and on the earthenware pots that decorate the house at festivals. To celebrate the spring, moreover, erotic clay statues are erected in the middle of each village. In India, as in every country in the world, protective power is attributed to erotic objects and to symbols and gestures with a phallic meaning. Some Shaivite sects, for example, require their devotees to wear a gold or silver lingam around their necks.

According to ancient Indian cosmology, in its ultimate reality, the universe is formed of interrelating forces in a substrate of pure energy. Whatever exists, from the atom to the most complex forms of life or thought, can be reduced to relations of numerical proportions. All that we term "aesthetic" is merely an intuitive perception of certain harmonies that in fact reveal the profound nature of things. Familiarity with the proportional factors we perceive in what we term "beauty" allows us to evoke and touch this essential nature, which is the very basis of creation.

The artist, the architect, becomes a magician. Through the power of magical diagrams or *yantras*, he reaches the source of being, the divine. The temple built according to the *yantras* thus allows us to evoke the invisible and communicate with those transcendent beings we call "gods."

Editor's Note:

The first part of this book, "Divine Eroticism," addresses the sometimes startling appearance of erotic symbolism in Hindu temples, linking it to the fundamental nature of existence and to the most ancient forms of philosophical and religious thought and practice. It also clarifies the role of erotic symbolism in evoking divine energy in temples and aiding mystical absorption in the cosmic substance of the universe.

The second part of the book, "Temples: Dwellings of the Gods," describes the process of temple siting and construction, the attributes of the temple architect, and the main elements of temple architecture, exploring in detail the symbolic meaning and power of each element that composes these divine dwelling places. Drawing on ancient architectural treatises, it reveals the magical-symbolic, mathematical-technical, and artistic aspects of Hindu temples.

The third part, "Revealing the Divine Mind," delves deeper into the iconography of the temples—its symbolism and ritualistic veneration—and its relationship to the human search for meaning and liberation.

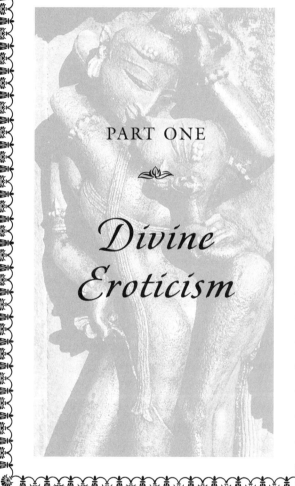

PART ONE

❧

*Divine
Eroticism*

The Nature of the World

When, in the neutral, formless cosmic substratum, there appears
the first tension that will give birth to the world, its aspect is
that of a polarization, or antinomy, containing a positive element and a negative element that repel and attract each other. From this tension is born orientation (the principle of space) and movement (the principle of time).
Space-time, or oriented movement, generates position, dimension, and duration. From the complex of oriented movements in space-time is born the
appearance of matter and its corollary, sensation. The substance of the universe is nothing but a tangle of oriented movements, located in the substratum of the cosmic mind, whose appearance—perceptible reality—is
produced by the limited perception of living beings. Indeed, our senses allow
us to perceive forms, sounds, colors, dimensions, and objects where there
are merely centers of energy separated by immense spaces. The macrocosm
and the microcosm, the Cosmic Being and living beings, the "creative" and
the "perceptive" are the indispensable complementary elements of manifes-
tation. By definition, therefore, microcosm and macrocosm, the one the
image and reflection of the other, consist of polarized tensions arising from
the repulsion of positive and negative elements.

The two mutually repellent poles—these two opposite tendencies that are
the principle of all creation, matter, form, sensation, and thought, inevitably
containing an active aspect and a passive aspect—are at a cosmic level called
Purusha (person) and Prakriti (nature). Their "mark" is found everywhere
and in all things. In ourselves, they find expression in the male and the
female organisms, strictly complementary and indispensable to one another.

*"The gods are
sixteen-year-old
adolescents."*

In describing the Primordial Cosmic Being, the *Upanishads* maintain that before creation these elements were not separate but were "clasped closely together like a man and woman" (*Brihadaranyaka Upanishad,* 1.4.3). When these two elements separate, a tension appears, which is the "desire to create" *(sisriksha)*. The state of repose or peace is thus represented by the union of opposites in a kind of continual coitus. Separation of the two poles creates instability, which gives rise to the creation of a universe of movement whose elements aspire toward union, to a merging into one another, to peace (their original and final state), to a state of total bliss and delight *(ananda)*—not to silence and death.

"He desired to be two. This is why [the person] divided himself in two parts. Thus man and woman appeared. This is why the body [of man] is like the half of a fruit. . . .Woman fills the void. And he unites with her" (*Brihadaranyaka Upanishad,* 1.4.3). The principle of our existence, and of all existence, is thus usually represented by the opposition of male and female and is symbolized by the organs that express this opposition. The uniting of these organs is the image of basic movement, the source of all existence and all life, removing the tension caused by the separation of positive and negative. "The symbols of the vulva and phallus represent the principles that cause the formation of the world. Their union expresses the nature of action" (*Vatula Shuddha Agama*). By their very nature, the forms of the organs that distinguish male and female are symbols. The universe knows no chance, no inconsistency. In choosing the erect phallus and the vulva as signs of divine causality, we are not attributing a symbolic meaning to an accidental anatomical form. It is the form itself that reveals to us an underlying aspect of the nature of things and of the Cosmic Person.

The uniting of the sexes is an expression of the nature of being that we envisage at a physical, mental, intellectual, subtle, or transcendent level. Upon reflection, it can reveal to us the secret of divine nature. All forms of such union, all the postures used in practicing it, all the variations to which it is subject, have a profound and magical meaning that in effect corresponds to the different potentialities of the created. The divine manifests itself directly in all procreation, in every creation, in all sensual delight.

"Of every kind of being, Universal Nature is the womb and I am the father who gives the seed" (*Bhagavad Gita,* 14.4). All other symbols are

The Divine Image

According to Hindu cosmological concepts, the world is a divine thought, a divine dream without substance, made only of elements of energy that manifest themselves as atoms, tendencies, and movements in what appears to us as matter, feeling, thought, consciousness, and life. The continuity and the interdependence of the various aspects of what we term "existence" or "reality" are absolute. Neither dimension nor duration exists as such. An instant lasts as long as an aeon; a molecule is not in the least smaller than a galaxy. The dimensions of space and time are defined only in relation to ourselves, to the wavelengths on which our tiny centers function as living beings.

To perceive states of existence wholly different from our own, therefore, we have merely to discard the limitations of the rhythmic power plant that determines our perceptions and dimension. The purpose of Yoga, for example, is to control the centers in charge of our various faculties, amplifying their sphere of activity and allowing us to return to the source from which they spring, thus escaping the metronome of time and space that imprisons us and restricts our perceptions.

The human being belongs to the terrestrial world and the Earth to the solar system. Nothing can exist—in the human being or on the Earth—the principle of which cannot be found in the solar system or in the galaxy to which it belongs. We have therefore a solar mind, a solar consciousness, solar perceptions, and a solar person acting.

If we manage to identify the coordinates that sum up the mechanisms corresponding to the functioning of our various faculties, symbolized by the

chakras (the energy centers, according to Yoga theory), we should discover the same data in all other aspects of the world. We should perceive that the stars are bound to each other by ties similar to those that exist between our subtle organs, whence the data of astrology and the relationship between star chart and *chakras*. Earth too has its energy centers that correspond to the same universal data and constitute centers of life and awareness. The study of such places is the subject of a special science known as sacred geography.

The temple, through which contacts or relations are established among the various states of being (among humans, spirits, and gods), is thus a combination of the data of Yoga, astrology, and sacred geography. In the temple structure, we find diagrams similar to the ones described for *chakras* according to Yoga experience, with proportions similar to those deriving from the position of the stars, by which their influence can be explained. Last come the characteristics of the site and orientation, which are connected to the living structure of the Earth.

The Hindu temple is thus not a place where the faithful may gather, but a sacred building constructed for the purpose of receiving subtle influences that are found in a place chosen for magical reasons. It is a kind of magnetic center, a *yantra* or "machine," which, thanks to its structure, crystallizes the cosmic energy irradiating around it. The temple is built on a diagram, a plan comprising various elements that give the building its own mysterious life. On the basis of this diagram, numbers, ratios, forms, and symbols are calculated according to precise rules, like the formulas used today to construct transistor receivers or nuclear reactors.

The activity of the temple is assured by priests—qualified magicians—who know all the appropriate formulas and rites to evoke the presence of a deity. Here the gods manifest themselves, and from here, prayers and the sacrificial smoke can reach them. In other words, the Hindu temple is a center of communication between two worlds that coexist and meet without recognition and without knowing anything of each other.

...oup composed of ...voman and three men (a king, a prince, and a servant). Their ...ositions form a ...eometric shape ...at corresponds to ...complex symbol with magical properties. ...itragupta Temple, Khajuraho, ...0th century C.E.

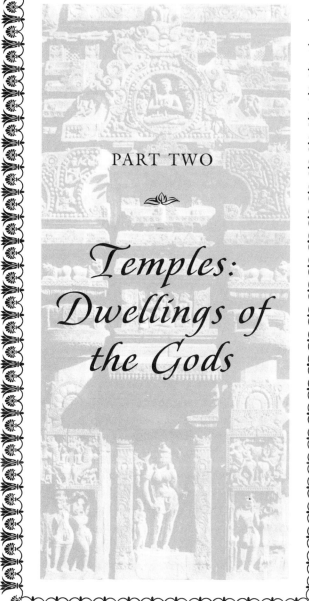

PART TWO

Temples:
Dwellings of
the Gods

Sacred Places

There exist privileged regions and places where energy—terrestrial magnetism—rises heavenward and where subtle, extraterrestrial, powers find a sort of chimney that allows them to descend to the world of human beings. Such places are called *tirtha* (ways), *kshetra* (fields), or *pitha*

Pilgrims alway manage to reac holy places, eve when those plac are now far fro inhabited areas lost in the fores Amarkantak, i Baghelkhand (central India), n the sources of th sacred rivers Sor Narmada, and Mahanadi.

The chariot of the
Sun driven by
Aruna, the deity of
the dawn. Bengal,
7th century.

to the *Samarangana Sutradhara,* the temples of Shiva or Vahni (Agni) are
built to the northeast; the temples of Surya, Vishnu, Indra, and Dharma are
built to the east; and those of Sanatkumar, Marut, and Savitri are built to
the southeast. The sanctuaries of Ganesha, of the Heavenly Mothers
(Matri), of the ghosts *(bhuta),* and of Death *(Yama)* lie to the south. The
temple of Bhadra Kali, the Great Goddess, is to the southwest; those of Vishvakarma (the architect of the gods), Prajapati (protector of animals), and
Varuna (lord of the waters) are to the west. The sanctuaries of the snakes
and of Saturn are built to the northwest, and those of Skanda (Beauty),
Soma (Immortality), and Kuvera (the lord of treasure) are to the north.

According to Hindu concepts, it is impossible to develop a harmonious civilization or live in a balanced manner in places that take no account of the laws of orientation and equilibrium connected to the nature of humans and of gods. A badly oriented temple is evil, and those who seek real contact with the gods fly from it in terror. The same is true of towns built without taking into account the laws of orientation that allow the various human groups to cooperate and live together in harmony.

The Temple Ground
and Preliminary Rites

A temple is always built near a river or pond. In the Rajputana desert, enormous water holes known as baori *were dug down to the water level, thus forming a small pool reached by stairs for the priests and faithful to make their ritual ablutions.*

Before being a building, a temple is essentially an isolated place, surrounded by a fence. Originally, the Roman *templum*—which gives us the word "temple"—indicated the square enclosure from which all external influences were excluded, within which the priests examined and interpreted the omens. In India too, we find the concept of the sacred enclosure known as the "dance floor," where the people gathered to invoke the gods

Temple of
Lakshmana,
Khajuraho,
10th century C.E.

Temple of
Kandariya
Mahadeva,
Khajuraho,
11th century C.E.

Temples:
Dwellings
of the Gods

through ecstatic dances, during which the "spirits" *(bhuta)* would possess a dancer and prophesy through his mouth. Similarly, the Temple of Heaven in China was a fenced enclosure where the emperor received inspiration from heaven. The same is also true of mosques, which were originally enclosed spaces open to the sky, and of Celtic churches, which even today are often still fenced around.

The plot of ground on which the temple is to be built has to be carefully tilled and leveled. The color of the soil has to be examined (white, red, yellow, or black), as well as its smell and taste (sweet, sour, bitter, or astringent). The color and taste of the soil determine the "caste" of the temple, i.e., the social group to which it will be particularly favorable. A hole is dug, ten inches (twenty-five centimeters) wide and one cubit (forty-five centimeters) deep, in which a lamp is lighted. If the flame goes out, the soil is bad. The humidity that collects during the night is then measured. Next, grain is sown: the time it takes to germinate will determine the quality of the location.

The unit of measurement used for temple construction is the thumb (the first phalanx) and the cubit (or "elbow" of the builder, taken as being the length of his forearm, from wrist to elbow). During all the magical building rites, the builder identifies himself with his work and is physically aware of any kind of error. Since the temple plan is similar to the shape of a human being *(vastu-purusha)*, it corresponds to the body of the architect himself, his various members thus being associated with the various energy centers *(chakras)* determined by Yoga.

The architect must then undergo a personal purification rite, together with those present at each stage of the building. The astrological data must also be consulted and favorable days taken into account, as well as the orientation and the position of the planets.

The Plan-Person
(*Vastu-Purusha*)

*O*n the temple plan, just as in a person's body, must be found the crucial points corresponding to the various subtle faculties defined by the Yoga *chakras*. These are the points where the universal person and the individual person meet. The temple plan is thus conceived as a diagram on which the various energy centers are located and is consequently known as the "plan-person" *(vastu-purusha)*.

The human chart of the temple, *vastu-purusha mandala,* is a magical diagram to be used by a qualified architect as the basis for building an efficacious temple. The *vastu-purusha* continues the tradition of the Vedic altar as far as the arrangement of its various members is concerned. The hands of the *purusha* are joined in the *anjali mudra,* the gesture of offering. Its position varies slightly according to whether the temple is built by a priest *(brahmana)* or a prince *(kshatriya).* In the first case, the head lies to the east, whereas in the other, to the north. In a temple built by a priest, the *vastu-purusha* stretches from east to west, following the sun's course, going from light to darkness.

The diagram on which the *vastu-purusha* is designed is obtained by dividing the temple plan into sixty-four or eighty-one squares (2^6 or 3^4). In these squares are represented forty-five deities corresponding to the members and vital organs of the *purusha.* The space set aside for each deity may vary, but not its respective position. In the center is situated the transcendent principle, *brahma sthana.* Twelve deities form the inner circle, surrounded by another thirty-two placed around the perimeter.

In Shaivite tradition, the *vastu-purusha* reposes on the golden serpent *(vastu-naga)*, which supports the Earth. Its vehicle is the bull. The serpent *(naga)* represents the nonmanifest aspect of Shiva and the bull his manifest aspect. In its anthropomorphic representation, the four-armed *vastu-purusha* holds a club, a trident, an axe, and a scepter adorned with a skull. It is red, like the rising sun.

The body of the *vastu-purusha* corresponds to that of the sacrificed human victim, on top of which the Vedic altar was built. The incorporation of the relics of a martyr in the Christian altar is also a survival of this practice. The lamb or goat is a replacement for the human victim (a symbol also found in the Christian *Agnus Dei* or "Lamb of God").

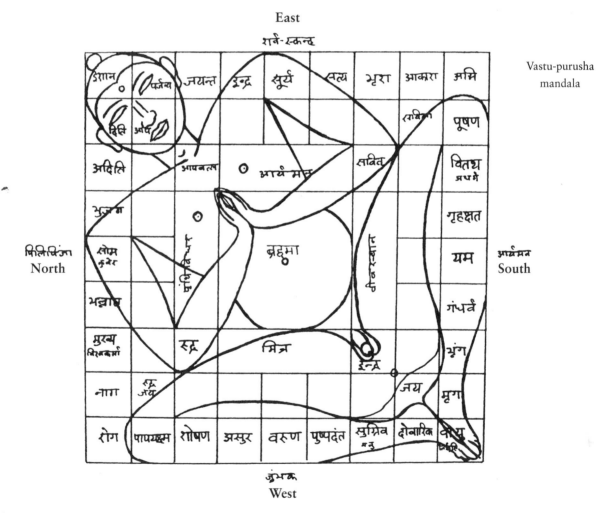

East

Vastu-purusha
mandala

North

South

West

As the general plan of the temple and the site, the *vastu-mandala* includes the power lines associated with the crossing of the *purusha's* subtle arteries, forming particularly sensitive points *(atimarma)* on which the temple's "health" depends. In the construction of the building, the lines of the *mandala* have to be rigorously observed so that no obstacle, column, support, or chapel can obstruct the circulation of living forces in the temple itself and in the surrounding area. This also has to be taken into account in establishing the axes, diagonals, openings, and other elements.

The subtle structure of the human body is not accidental. It summarizes the possibilities of existence in a given world and reflects laws that are valid for the individual, for society, and for the transcendental world of the gods. Life's scenario must be suited to human nature and become an extension of the human being. It must be in harmony with cosmic laws, not mock them. The whole universe is governed by proportional ratios and numerical relations. Human structures—whether temples, palaces, houses, or cities—must harmonize and integrate with the natural order, because otherwise people will not be at ease there, and evil tendencies will take over.

Erotic Representations

The outer and inner walls of the Hindu temple are entirely covered with symbolic representations and sculptures describing the various aspects of earthly and heavenly life in which erotic scenes prevail. Since this fact often arouses great surprise, it is best to clarify their significance and explain why such portrayals are present in holy places while excluding a priori any pornographic connotation.

The value of the erotic representations decorating Hindu temples is both magical and educational. The various forms of the union of opposites are situated at crucial points in the temple structure and form part of its meaning as the image of the cosmic world. The use of several figures means that highly complex diagrams can be employed, which have a greater magical effect. The position of the images sculpted on the walls, columns, vaulting, and doors of the temple is determined by each image's own diagram as well as by the place it must occupy within the overall plan of the temple. The major erotic groups constructed on a square diagram occupy the center of the northern and southern façades. The center of the west wall is occupied by an image of the Sun, the temple's entrance being to the east.

To create an image, the sculptors first trace its diagram or *yantra* on the stone using an awl, carefully observing the proportions of the various linear elements. Then, at the points shown on the diagram, they indicate the body's structural centers as defined by Yoga principles—wrists, ankles, the base of the neck, navel, sexual organ, knees, etc.—after which the image is sculpted in relief.

These sculptures recount the development of every kind of erotic relation.

Background: Pilgrims at Konarak Temple.
Photograph by Bernard Bazinet

Top inset: Carving of Narasimha
(man-lion), one of Vishnu's incarnations, on
stone pillar at Vittala Temple, Karnataka State,
16th century. Photograph by Nancy Yeilding

Bottom inset: Dancing apsara from the thousand
pillar hall, Meenakshi Temple, Madurai.
Photograph by Ehud C. Sperling

Background: Apsaras, Adinath Temple (Jain temple), Khajuraho, 11th century. Photograph by Jacques E. Cloarec

Top inset: Erotic sculptures on the capitals of the Nepalese wood temple, Varanasi. Photograph by Jacques E. Cloarec

Bottom inset: Detail of gopis, temple outside Madurai. Photograph by Ehud C. Sperling

Background: Temple of Meenakshi interior central pond and tower, Madurai. Photograph by Ehud C. Sperling

Top inset: Carved column inside old temple on Hemakuta Hill, Karnataka State, circa 8th century. Photograph by Nancy Yeilding

Bottom inset: Stone relief of Hanuman, Vittala Temple, Karnataka State, 16th century. Photograph by Nancy Yeilding

Top: *Rama, Lakshmana, and Sita, Vittala Temple, Vijayanagar,
Karnataka State, 16th century. Photograph by Nancy Yeilding*

Bottom: Mithuna, *Vishvanatha Temple dedicated to Shiva, Khajuraho,
10th century. Photograph by Jacques E. Cloarec*

Inset: *Parsvanatha Temple (Jain temple), Khajuraho, 10th century.
Photograph by Jacques E. Cloarec*

Background: Apsara carved into temple pillar, ruins of Vijayanagar, Karnataka State. Photograph by Nancy Yeilding

Top inset: Divyangana, Duladeo Temple dedicated to Shiva, Khajuraho, 10th century. Photograph by Jacques E. Cloarec

Bottom inset: Carving of temple dancer, Vittala Temple, Karnataka State, 16th century. Photograph by Nancy Yeilding

Top: Arial view of Achyutarya Temple,
Vijayanagar, Karnataka State.
Photograph by Nancy Yeilding

Bottom: Kandariya Mahadeva Temple, Khajuraho,
11th century. Photograph by Jacques E. Cloarec

Inset: Mithuna, Vishvanatha Temple dedicated
to Shiva, Khajuraho, 10th century.
Photograph by Jacques E. Cloarec

Background: One of the most beautiful shikharas from the West group at Khajuraho. Photograph by Jacques E. Cloarec

Top inset: Apsaras, Adinath Temple (Jain temple), Khajuraho, 11th century. Photograph by Jacques E. Cloarec

Bottom inset: Temple of Meenakshi, Madurai. Photograph by Ehud C. Sperling

*Background: Krishna Temple, Vijayanagar, Karnataka
State. Photograph by Nancy Yeilding*

*Inset: Krishna Temple, Vijayanagar, Karnataka State.
Photograph by Nancy Yeilding*

Temple sculptures represent every aspect of amorous relations. Here a lover is about to strip a hesitant young woman of her skimpy clothes. Temple of Raja-rani, Bhuvaneshvar, 12th century C.E.

We see first approaches, kisses, hands slipping beneath clothing, and manual stimulation performed by men, women, or children, either on themselves or on some partner. Penetration includes every imaginable posture, some of which are quite acrobatic, requiring the help of assistants. The representations include oral intercourse, cunnilingus, sodomy, solitary or group masturbation, and so on.

Images of women copulating with animals are frequently represented, whereas female homosexual practices are rare, except for those involving

Opposite:
Base of column
with erotic scenes
and childbirth.
Barmer, Rajputana,
12th century C.E.

A Kama Sutra
posture. Temple of
Lakshmana,
Khajuraho,
10th century C.E.

young girls. Scenes of male homosexuality always show at least one character wearing monastic garb. Most of the erotic images represent gods or demigods wearing crowns. The portrayal of human beings is more realistic, less stylized, and less idealized than that of the gods.

Opposite:
Base of column
with various scenes.
Barmer, Rajputana,
12th century C.E.

The Building of the Temple

*T*he temple is above all an abstract structure, corresponding to the power lines established on the plan and in space. Its reality lies in its proportions and measurements. The temple's visual aspect, its solid material, is merely a "covering." In this sense, it corresponds to an astrological chart or to the proportions inherent in the nature of the living being. Considered from this point of view, the temple is called *vi-mana* (that which is measured). It reproduces the inner rhythms of the human being and of the world, besides the deities who correspond to these rhythms: Agni (Fire), Vata (Wind), Surya (Sun), etc. During construction, each brick or stone is identified with the divine aspect corresponding to its setting with the aid of *mantras,* magic formulas with a meter that evokes the rhythmic element under consideration. The science of numbers *(ganita)* makes it possible to establish relations between the various forms of existence and to evoke them in the temple structures. Since it becomes the residence of a deity, the temple is then called *prasada* (seat), *dvalaya* (house of god), or simply *mandira* (dwelling).

Once a suitable site has been identified for the temple and has been dedicated with rites and sacrifices, it is carefully cleaned, purified, and fenced. The architect will then establish the unit of measurement that will serve to determine proportions. Typically, he will choose between his own cubit and the king's. Sometimes, however, he will adopt a wholly different basic measurement, because, as with musical harmony, only proportional ratios of the temple are important, not the dimensions.

Next to be built is the high platform on which the temple will rest, called

*...s-relief showing
...e building of a
...mple, Konarak.*

jagati (world). Its width must be three or four times that of the *prasada,* the temple itself. On this platform, the temple is built up to the level known as *kati* (the hip), corresponding to the height of the entrance stairs leading to where the sanctuary and the image to be worshiped will be located. On the platform, at the point identified on the central axis, is marked the place where the sanctuary will be located.

Temples:
Dwellings
of the Gods

48

The Sanctuary
(*Garbha Griha*)

The sanctuary is called *garbha griha* (dwelling of the embryo). The *hiranya garbha* (golden embryo) is the creative power from which the universe issues, and the *garbha griha* is the "matrix" in which it manifests. It also corresponds to the cavity in the human heart where the immensity of the principle (the *brahman*) is hidden.

The sanctuary is located at the center of the temple, and its only opening faces east. The most ancient Hindu sanctuaries are flat stone *dolmen*s, vertical and horizontal slabs forming a square room at the center of a stone wall boundary. Dating from prehistoric times, *dolmens* are still constructed today among the Himalayan populations, as well as among primitive Indian tribes, particularly the Gonds. The *dolmen* is the essence of the temple. However vast and imposing the temple structures may be, their splendor serves solely as an ornament to this small bare tabernacle in which the deity is manifest.

The *garbha griha* is a cube-shaped room, without decoration, which reproduces the original *dolmen*. As a rule, it is covered by a flat stone. On the architrave are sculpted the images of the nine planets (*nava-graha*). Only a qualified priest may enter this magical place to worship the image with flowers, water, lights, incense, and offerings symbolizing the five elements. There is often a totally secret and wholly closed *garbha griha*, located beneath the visible one containing the *linga* used for the rites and for worship.

The sanctuary of Chhapri Temple seen from the circular mandala. Central India, th century C.E.

49

*Door of the
sanctuary in the
Dasavatara
Temple at
Deogarh in
central India,
7th century* C.E.

A narrow passage runs around the sanctuary, to be walked along clockwise, so that the temple or monument is on one's right, except in Tantric rites of black magic. Walking counterclockwise is considered to be maleficent.

*The guardian of the
door of the
sanctuary
at the Dasavatara
Temple at Deogarh,
7th century* C.E.

A World Apart

The raised platform on which the temple is built represents an altar, on which the temple itself symbolizes all the aspects of ritual sacrifice. It comprises five small sanctuaries, four at the corners and one, dedicated to Shiva's vehicle, the bull, in front of the entrance. The bull is represented standing. Both men and women touch its testicles to obtain fertility.

During the great period of Indian architecture, from the ninth to the

Remains of a circular mandapa. *Temple of Kiradu, Rajputana, 12th century* C.E.

fourteenth century, temples were veritable small towns, surrounded by a wall and including, around the main sanctuary, many smaller sanctuaries. There were great pools for ablutions, halls with even one thousand columns, and platforms for spectacles. Dancing and the theater are the subject of the fifth Veda, since they are the means of teaching the people the legends of the gods and the virtues of the heroes. The theater thus belongs to temple activities. Female dancers also play a role in sacred prostitution, so essential to social equilibrium.

The merchants, however, had to stay outside the walls, where the priests—as well as the dancers and musicians attached to the temple—had their residences. The problem of keeping merchants out of the temple did not only concern the temple of Jerusalem.

In southern India it is still possible to see these various enclosure walls, which make the temple a world apart, peopled by gods, priests, and crowds of the faithful.

The Origin of Temple Forms

*T*he various temple structures appear to have different origins. In India, *dolmens* of flat standing stones, covered by wide slabs, have existed from prehistoric times, marking sacred places and the presence of deities. *Menhirs,* which are *lingas* (signs), also serve to call attention to the sacred nature of a site. They are phallic emblems and are also erected as ex-votos in places that have already been consecrated, their function being to delimit the sacred area.

The Vedic initiation hut—made of four bamboo poles stuck in the ground, tied together at the top, and covered with plaited banana and palm leaves—could be another of the original elements and may have inspired the curved shape of the *shikhara*. The design of the Vedic altar, similar to the brick-built Greek altar, has also had a decisive role in the conception of the *vastu-purusha*.

Lastly, the chariot, the vehicle of the gods: Each temple is likened to a chariot, whose immobility is only apparent. Sometimes, as at the Temple of the Sun at Konarak, enormous stone wheels create the illusion of an immense chariot bearing the temple itself. To carry the gods' images in procession, temple-shaped cars are built, drawn by the faithful.

According to the *Agni Purana,* the gods travel on five kinds of flying chariot: square, rectangular, round, elliptical, and octagonal. As the vehicles of the gods, the temples have the same form as their cars. Thus, all five forms are allowed in building a temple. Since there are theoretically nine variations to each of these forms, forty-five different kinds of temple are possible (*Agni Purana*, 104.11–21). According to the *Samarangana Sutradhara* (49.22–202), there are sixty-four types of temple: twenty-four square types for Brahma, ten

rectangular types for Shiva, ten circular types for Kuvera, ten elliptical types for Varuna, and ten octagonal ones for Indra.

As far as architectural styles are concerned, temples are divided into three categories: Nagara, Dravida, and Vesara. The Nagara style is universal, whereas the Dravida is the ancient style, found in southern India, and the Vesara (mule) is a hybrid mixture of the other two. In the Nagara style the tower is curved, whereas it is pyramidal in Dravida architecture. These different conceptions of temple architecture seem to have their origin in the two great traditions that form Indian civilization. The first is the protohistorical Shaivite and Dravidian civilization, whose gods are the *asuras* and whose architect is Maya, and the second is the Vedic-Aryan civilization, whose gods are called the *suras* and whose great architect is Vishvakarma, the artificer of the universe.

A Dravida type of shikhara. *Temple of Mallikarjuna, Pattadakal, Mysore, 7th century* C.E.

Temple of the Nagara type, Pattadakal, Mysore.

Architectural Treatises

*T*he *Vastu Shastra,* which is a treatise on architecture, is considered to be an *upa-Veda,* a "secondary" Veda, belonging—like all the magical sciences *(Tantras)*—to the *Atharva Veda* (the science of subtle correspondence). The art of building is closely connected to astrology, since the temple evokes the structure of the astral world, and the orientation of all its elements is tied to the forces and stars that determine the directions of space.

Architecture thus has a magical-symbolical aspect, a mathematical-technical aspect, and an artistic and craftwork element. The theoretical, magical, and symbolic aspects are described in the *Vastu Shastras* and in the *Tantras,* and the technical and artistic aspects are found in the *Shilpa Shastras,* which are the builders' and artisans' manuals. Architecture is, however, more particularly connected with astrology *(jyotisha)* and to ritual *(kalpa),* since the temple is the center of rites and sacrifices.

PART THREE

Revealing
the
Divine Mind

The Images of the Gods

"The body (akriti) *of the temple represents*
Prakriti, primordial nature."

Agni Purana, 61.25

In Shaivite temples (dedicated to Shiva) the image is a *linga,* an erect phallus. In the temples dedicated to other gods, they are represented anthropomorphically, always in a standing position. The principal images of the gods are placed inside recesses, called *ghana dvara* (blind doors). These niches form passages for magical inflows and are not doors for human beings.

Apsaras. *Temple of Mukteshvara, Bhuvaneshvar, 11th century* C.E.

Background: Main tower, temple of Meenakshi, Madurai.
Photograph by Ehud C. Sperling

Top inset: Mithuna, Devi-Jagadambi Temple dedicated to Parvati,
Khajuraho, 10th century. Photograph by Jacques E. Cloarec

Bottom inset: Ganesha stone carving, ruins of Vijayanagar,
Karnataka State. Photograph by Nancy Yeilding

Background: Kandariya Mahadeva Temple belonging to the West group at Khajuraho, 11th century. Photograph by Jacques E. Cloarec

Top inset: Vishnu carving at Vittala Temple, Karnataka State, 16th century. Photograph by Nancy Yeilding

Bottom inset: Dancing apsara and two musicians with drums. Parsvanatha Temple (Jain temple), Khajuraho, 10th century. Photograph by Jacques E. Cloarec

Top: Temple surrounded by water at foot of Matunga Hill,
Vijayanagar, Karnataka State. Photograph by Nancy Yeilding

Inset: Sexual activities with a horse, Lakshmana Temple,
Khajuraho, 10th century. Photograph by Jacques E. Cloarec

Bottom: The temple of Konarak, conceived of as a gigantic
chariot of the Sun God, 13th century.
Photograph by Bernard Bazinet

Background: Yakshini welcoming the bhaktas *(devotees) at the entrance of a temple, now a ruin in the outskirts of Madurai. Photograph by Ehud C. Sperling*

Top inset: Two lovers, Javari Temple, Khajuraho, 10th century. Photograph by Jacques E. Cloarec

Bottom inset: Temple ruins, Vijayanagar, Karnataka State. Photograph by Nancy Yeilding

Background: Hanuman (monkey-god, from the Ramaana), Hazara Rama Temple, Vijayanagar, Karnataka State. Photograph by Nancy Yeilding

Top inset: Detail of Krishna, temple outside Madurai. Photograph by Ehud C. Sperling

Bottom inset: Adinath Temple (Jain temple), Khajuraho, 11th century. Photograph by Jacques E. Cloarec

Top left: Shiva holding a trident, temple at Khajuraho. Photograph by Jacques E. Cloarec

Top right: Decorative ceiling, temple of Meenakshi, Madurai. Photograph by Ehud C. Sperling

Bottom: Krishna and gopis at a temple outside Madurai. Photograph by Ehud C. Sperling

Background: Stone lion carved in pillar, Vittala Temple, 16th century. Photograph by Nancy Yeilding

Top inset: Shikharas at the temple at Jageshvar, Uttar Pradesh, 7th century. Photograph by Nancy Yeilding

Bottom inset: Young women performing a puja in front of the linga at the Duladeo Temple dedicated to Shiva, Khajuraho, 10th century. Photograph by Jacques E. Cloarec

Top: Mithuna, *Kandariya Mahadeva Temple,
Khajuraho, 11th century.*
Photograph by Jacques E. Cloarec

Bottom: *Lakshmana Temple, Khajuraho, 10th century.*
Photogaph by Jacques E. Cloarec

Inset: *Dancing* apsara, *Duladeo Temple dedicated
to Shiva, Khajuraho, 10th century.*
Photograph by Jacques E. Cloarec

va and Parvati.
Temple of
shurameshvara,
buvaneshvar,
b century C.E.

divine converge. No action lacks the feeling of divine reality. Each one of life's actions, all beauty and voluptuousness, becomes a ritual action, a contact with the supernatural. This gives every act of love and every experience of beauty its true dimension and its unrivaled intensity. The human action and the divine action become one.

The Three Gods

phallic Shiva in
sana (the Yoga
ure). Seated on
tus flower, he
olds a club
dowed with
n eye and
urrounded by
assistants, the
as. Temple of
ukteshvara,
uvaneshvar,
century C.E.

According to Hindu cosmology, the origin of all things was a vast expanding centrifugal force or explosion, which today we call the "big bang." The principle of this explosion that gives birth to the world is called Shiva. This original force is offset by the power of coagulation, a centripetal force generating energy centers, suns, and atoms. This latter force is nature (Prakriti), the origin of worlds. It is called Shakti (energy) if it is considered as the female counterpart of Shiva, or Vishnu (the omnipresent) if envisaged as a male principle. The symbols of Shakti and Vishnu are interchangeable. The balance of these two forces gives rise to circular motion, the organization of atoms, solar systems, and galaxies. This organizing principle that gives rise to matter, to the measurable notions of space and time, is called Brahma (greatness).

We find the balance or opposition of these three elements in every aspect of the world, at all levels (material, vital, intellectual, and spiritual). The three gods—Brahma, Vishnu, and Shiva, who oppose and complete each other in the reality of the world—represent this trinity. No single one of them can exist without the others, but they cannot be reduced to one. Oneness is not a principle. It is created by the union of several elements. In the human, as in all things, it is the union of opposites—the sexual act—that constitutes oneness. Each human individual is only one half—or in fact, one third—since it is the spark of joy, voluptuousness, and experience of the divine state that constitutes the third element, humankind's raison d'être.

Coupling *(Mithuna)*

The total union of the two basic principles, the person (Purusha) and nature (Prakriti), is likened to that of "a man and a woman closely entwined." The union of the individual with the total being—the human with the divine—is also likened to the union of the couple. The very image of the final purpose of all existence, reintegration with the whole, is thus identified with the act of love:

> Just as a man closely entwined with the woman he desires no longer distinguishes the outside from the inside, so the man who embraces the divine no longer distinguishes between outside and inside. In it he finds his real form, the one that satisfies his desire, the supreme being who is all that is desirable. Desire and pain exist no more.
>
> (*Brihadaranyaka Upanishad,* 4.3.21)

The temple's purpose is to draw the human closer to the divine, to create a passage, a bond between the two. This purpose finds its expression in the portrayal of the act of union through which the wandering individual finds fullness and totality in uniting with that half of oneself from which one felt separated. Everywhere, at all the main points of the temple—and even at the entrance to the sanctuary—we find the act of love represented, not at all as a reproductive act but as an act of voluptuousness, of full self-realization in the joy of refinding self.

It is not merely a symbolic portrayal. A person is never truly whole, never really himself or herself, never really close to the divine, except in the

Mithuna, a m
diagram of an
nature. Temp
Vishvanath
Khajuraho
10th century

i (Fire) receiving va's sperm, the ciple of life. The universe is a etual sacrificial ite, in which ity—Fire—exists y by destroying We can live only devouring other ing beings, and we participate in Cosmic Sacrifice. huvaneshvar, h century C.E.

Skanda (jet of sperm)— also called Kumara (virgin boy), Kartikeya (the Pleiades' suckling), or Subrahmanyam (dear to the Brahmans)—was born of Shiva's sperm and has no mother. He is the god of beauty, chief of the heavenly army. His vehicle is the peacock. He has no wife, and his cult is forbidden to women. Temple of Mukteshvara, Bhuvaneshvar, 9th century C.E.

made manifest by their union. Thus, Shiva and Shakti each have a son, but their children were born independently. Shiva's son is called Skanda (the jet of sperm). He is the god of beauty and war, captain of the gods' army. Skanda was born when, during the sacrifice that gave rise to the world,

Revealing the Divine Mind

Shiva poured his own sperm as a ritual offering into the mouth of Agni, the Fire. Unable to withstand the potency of the divine seed, Agni had to spit it out. It fell into the Ganges, the sacred river of knowledge, which bore the divine sperm to rest in a reedy marsh. There Skanda grew up, fed by the seven Pleiades. He grew seven heads in order to drink their milk. He became the god of beauty, the perfect adolescent. He refuses all contact with women, remaining a virgin, or at least eschewing relations with female beings. His cult and his temples are forbidden to women. His only spouse is the army *(sena)*.

The son of Parvati is called Ganapati, or Ganesha. He is the god of quantities and has an elephant's head. He removes all obstacles and must be worshiped before undertaking any enterprise. Parvati, who wanted a guardian for her door, scraped the dirt from her body while bathing and formed a ball to which she gave life with her breath. This is how the astute elephant-god was born. He grew quickly and fought furiously against Shiva's guards. Later on, he took two wives: Siddhi (Successful Outcome) and Riddhi (Success).

Shiva's symbol may be replaced, according to the religious notions of the faithful, by images of the other two gods (Brahma or Vishnu/Shakti) or by those of secondary deities deriving from them and presenting less abstract aspects, which are closer and more accessible. Thus there are temples of Indra (the king of heaven), the Sun (source of light), Skanda (beauty), Ganesha (the oneness of the human and the divine), Shakti (the female principle in its various forms), and the various aspects and incarnations of Vishnu (the lion-man, Rama, Krishna, etc.).

The *Linga*, Shiva's Phallic Emblem

The symbolic image worshiped in the sanctuary of the temple of Shiva consists of three parts: a cubic altar surmounted by the female emblem—*arghya* (receptacle) or *yoni* (female organ)—that serves as a container and outlet for the lustral water. Grasped in the center of the *yoni* is the *linga* (phallus), Shiva's emblem. It is sculpted from a square stone within the altar. The part that passes through the *yoni* is octagonal, whereas the part that rises above the altar is cylindrical, surrounded by a snake that licks the extremity with its forked tongue.

The altar represents the world, creation as a whole, born from the union of opposites—from the phallus, source of life and intellect, and the womb, symbol of cosmic energy. In Shiva's symbol, however, the phallus neither penetrates the vulva nor loses itself inside the vagina for the purpose of fecundating. On the contrary, clenched at its base by the *yoni,* it frees itself to rise toward the zenith.

Virile power, the principle that fecundates and disposes, is the source of organized life and intelligence. The seminal energy poured into the receptacle, or female organ, gives birth to life, the harmony of forms. Once freed from its female aspect, however, this energy becomes the substance of the intellect. Intelligence, which in the macrocosm creates the world's forms and in the microcosm perceives order and death, is an essentially male principle. Woman participates in it as a result of a reflex of intelligence to the extent that she too, like all beings, is androgynous. At the level of creation, all elements participate

*Through his cosmic dance, Shiva creates the forms of the spatial world. His twelve arms
symbolize his dominion over time. The snake represents the cycle of aeons, the trident the
destructive power of time in the three worlds. Shiva's spouse, the Power of Time (Kali) is
armed with a club. In this ithyphallic representation of the god, Shiva's vehicle, the bull,
licks his testicles. Bearing garlands, Shiva's servants, the* ganas, *are seen flying
on either side of the medallion, surrounded by a rosary of* rudraksha *seeds
(the eyes of Shiva), which are sacred to him. Temple of Vaital-deul,
Bhuvaneshvar, 9th century* C.E.

in both principles and are a mixture of male and female. In the microcosm, or body, it is possible to observe this ambivalence. Every cell of our body contains positive and negative elements and is thus, to a differing degree, bisexual.

The spermatozoid substance placed in the female has a fecundating action, but the same substance, when reabsorbed through sexual abstinence, nourishes the cerebral matter. Rising, according to the Yogic formula, through the subtle channels flanking the backbone, it renders the intellectual faculties more acute. The Yogi perceives sexual energy as though it were coiled up at the base of the spine, which is why it is called *kundalini* (coiled) and likened to a sleeping snake. When, by means of mental concentration, it awakens and unwinds its coils, it rises like a column of fire toward the zenith, toward the top of the skull—the image of the heavenly vault—and pierces it to reach the transcendent worlds. Shiva's liberated phallus represents this illuminating power rising heavenward, beyond the material world and its door, which is the *yoni* or female organ. In this case, the *linga* is likened to a pillar of light.

Shardula at
Khajuraho,
10th century C.E.

Shardula at
Konarak,
14th century C.E.

Revealing the
Divine Mind

The Power of Nature, Shardula

꧁꧁꧁꧁꧁꧁꧁꧁꧁꧁

The lion, Shardula, is the symbol of the power of nature, Prakriti, the female principle through which Shiva (Purusha) becomes manifest. Without this energy through which he manifests himself, Shiva is like a lifeless body *(shava)*. The perceptible world is the work of Maya, the power of illusion, which makes it appear to be real. This appearance of reality is called Prakriti (nature). All that exists is the work and the domain of Prakriti. All that lives is in the power of nature.

In a small sanctuary in front of the temple entrance or in front of the *shikhara* and dominating the *mandapa* (the world of the living) is placed the image of the power of nature, Shardula, the lion. Between the lion's paws is a little man bearing a sword. This is the Yogi who, armed with the sword of knowledge, is the only one able to overcome the power of nature and free himself from the chains of existence. With knowledge, the Yogi can attain liberation, returning to the causal principle that is Shiva.

Apsaras and *Gandharvas*

The *apsaras* are nymphs of paradise, deities of lakes and springs. In Hindu mythology, they represent potential, unrealized worlds. Not all the universes dreamed of by the creator materialize. Each of them is portrayed as a nymph of dazzling beauty. Such dreams are the amusements of the gods. They sometimes send them to sages to distract them from their

Gandharva flying.
Temple of
Khajuraho,
10th century C.E.

austere meditations and to prevent them from freeing themselves from the ties of the world, since "all living creatures are useful to the gods, just as cattle are useful to humanity. Even if one beast is taken, it is unpleasant. This is why the gods are displeased that men should gain knowledge" (*Brihadaranyaka Upanishad*, 1.4.10).

The heavenly beauties are innumerable. Always ready to seduce, they are sculpted at every corner of the temple, both inside and outside. They are called "water nymphs" *(apsaras),* "heavenly beauties" *(surasundaris),* or even "hetaeras of heaven" *(svarveshyas).* The *apsaras* dance for the delight of gods and men. Their male counterparts are the *gandharvas* (celestial musicians), who are seen floating in the air and playing various instruments.

The *vidyadharas* (bringers of wisdom) are the warriors of heaven. Armed with scimitars, they fend the air when they go to combat ignorance. They are symbolically associated with *pranayama,* the Yogic breath control, or other means used by the sage to take possession of himself and begin his

*Revealing the
Divine Mind*

battle against the forces of nature, against the ignorance that chains him to the endless cycle of existence.

The *ganas* are a separate group of heavenly beings. Adolescent servants of Shiva, they are the rascals of heaven, running about here and there in search of trouble or some trick to play on gods and humans. These enfants terribles are also the tools of justice. Courageous and generous, they fight against all false morals, hypocrisy, and convention. They rob the rich to feed the poor and mock the pretensions of gods and the ambitions of human beings. Like all Shiva's servants, they are champions of the oppressed, the humble, and the despised. Proud and quarrelsome, they can be heard on stormy nights as they prepare some dirty trick.

Ethics and Sexuality

*H*indu legislators distinguish two kinds of fundamentally different kinds of ethic: the personal, aimed to perfect the individual, and the social, understood as the body of practical rules aiming to regulate the collectivity.

For human equilibrium, realization on the erotic level is an ineluctable necessity. Owing to the complexity of their structure, human beings present an almost infinite variety of differences. It is therefore impossible to establish rules aiming to limit individual moral behavior without risking the persecution of individuals who, as human beings, not only have the right but also the duty of realizing their own nature, both physically and mentally. Persons whose psychological and physiological balance is harmed run the risk, owing to lack of stability, of being unable to realize their own spiritual destiny. The person must free himself or herself from what he or she has desired, loved, and accomplished so as to be able to reach the true freedom of nonaction and then of nonbeing. The Hindus have consequently never been able or wished to establish an individual moral code. The first duty of every person is toward oneself. One must therefore live so to realize whatever one most deeply desires in order to be able to free oneself from it subsequently.

The need to maintain a social framework, on the other hand, necessitates the creation of a code of ethics, including the inevitable prohibitions. A precise distinction has to be made between such purely technical and human restrictions based on common interest and the individual ethic, which has quite another aim. Hindu legislators have incontestably sought to establish a society that respects the human being's double nature, as both individual and social being. In India's multiracial reality and with its highly developed society inevitably stratified by the existence of the caste system, the purpose of marriage has been to guarantee the continuation of ethnic and professional groups. It is a fundamental social institution based on common interests. Traditionally, marriages were therefore arranged within the professional or ethnic group during early adolescence, when sexuality is easily fixated on available objects.

Most individuals are happy with a limited erotic life if it begins early enough. As foreseen by the Hindu system, polygamy offers men the possibility of renovation. For women, on the other hand, maternity is usually the main center of interest, and eroticism consequently occupies a very secondary role. Nevertheless, a sensual woman may count on a certain tolerance, tacitly granted, for her infidelities with certain members of her family group (cousins, brothers-in-law, uncles, nephews, etc.). This system, which is very widespread in India, causes no damage to either race or caste and, as a rule, offers sufficient opportunity to satisfy the sensual woman. Manu, the lawgiver, recommends this kind of family adjustment in the event of a sterile marriage (*Manu Smriti*, 9.59).

From a social point of view, marrying out of caste or outside the racial group is an absolutely unpardonable betrayal, and the woman is excluded from her social environment. For women who are unwilling to accept restrictions, however, special professions are provided, particularly the theater, music, and dancing. Women inclined to adventure or born outside the social frame find in such professions (which imply a certain degree of prostitution) a pleasant, adventurous, and easy life. These trades, as also prostitution itself, are confirmed by law and have a sacred character, placed under the protection of the temples. Until the eighteenth century, the numerous residential annexes of some temples sheltered several thousand carefully educated prostitute dancers or musicians, who made a considerable contribution to the maintaining of social order. Since sexuality was neither discredited nor despised, but on the contrary, presented and taught as one of the fine arts, it was considered a legitimate and honorable calling. It needed no pretext, such as the often false pretence of love, to lend legitimacy to the exercise of a basic physical function and explain the scope of the most important of the arts of pleasure.

Play between a young woman and a little girl. Temple of Raja-rani, Bhuvaneshvar, 12th century C.E.

According to the *Matsya Purana,* a woman who has had several lovers, and is thus relegated to the rank of a prostitute, must follow a certain amorous discipline to please the gods and deserve paradise. Such a woman must:

Worship Vishnu, the refuge of men, represented as the god of love.
On touching the feet of his image, she must say, "I worship him who desires;"
on touching his hips, "I worship what makes us lose our head;"
on touching his sexual organ, "I worship the source of passion;"
on touching his navel, "I worship the ocean of pleasure;"
on touching his belly, "I worship what seduces me;"
on touching his heart, "I worship the master of my soul;"
on touching his breast, "I worship the cause of my joys;"
on touching his neck, "I worship what disturbs me;"
on touching his face, "I worship what makes me happy;"
on touching his left side, "I worship him whose bow is made of flowers (Eros);"
on touching his right side, "I worship him whose arrows are made of flowers;"
on touching his forehead, "I worship the dwelling of the spirit;"
on touching his hair, "I worship infidelity, inconstancy;"
on touching his whole body, "I worship him who is the soul of all things."
"I salute him who knows no anguish and who brings happiness. In him I salute tenderness, desire, beauty, strength, satisfaction, the possession of all goods."

The woman who has thus worshiped the powerful god of love must invite to her home a *brahman* learned in the sacred books whose body is without defects. She shall offer him flowers, sandalwood, a bushel of rice, a pot of butter, and shall say to him, "May the bridegroom of Fortune be satisfied."

In her heart considering him as divine Eros, she shall with pleasure do whatever he asks her. She shall place herself at his disposal smiling and with all her soul. She shall perform this rite every Sunday for thir-

Erotic composition of a princely figure with three favorites. Temple of Vishvanatha, Khajuraho, 10th century C.E.

individual existence will continue in some "almost human" form or as some kind of asexual angel. Sexuality is the key to our biological role and human personality, as it is to our transmigrating entity itself and to our destiny. We must respect it and honor it to the day when we no longer need it, until we can abandon it together with everything connected with it—that is, whatever concerns our very existence. If sexuality manages to keep its secrets from us, it will play games with us, and at the very moment when we boast of having freed ourselves from it, we shall be all the more firmly in its grasp.

The chastity practiced by Yogis transforms sexual energy into mental power. It is a difficult technique but gives considerable and rapid results. It cannot be realized without contemplating the divine phallus, without concentrating on the subtle centers of eroticism in our own body. Chastity is not a virtue but a technique. The man who practices abstinence at all costs, incapable of dominating his own secretions and his own dreams, is only fooling himself. The more he tries to banish and escape from it, the more sexuality controls his secret impulses, inevitably impregnating his sub-conscious activities, playing games with him, and forcibly enslaving him. Puritanism is the surest obstacle to liberation, the most terrible impediment a person can encounter in the search for the divine.

It is clear that only the ambitious, the rapacious, the cruel, and the unsatisfied fear the manifestations of sexuality. Fear of sexuality has always been an indication of antispirituality. Demoniac sovereigns persecute sexuality, so that in becoming more secret it henceforth controls not only the body, which is of little importance, but also the mind. This it perverts in complexes, in sentimental substitutes, dissimulating it in forms of religion or social service, and thus upsetting values to such an extent that none can escape from it any longer.

The temples are covered with erotic images because human beings have to be pure and free from inhibitions before they can grasp the secrets of knowledge. The wise person does not fear the spectacle of pleasure but instead admires its splendor and beauty. According to the Shaivite *Puranas* and the *Tantras,* only those who worship the phallus, who adore the Creator in the most naked and guileless form of the procreative organ, may hope to overcome nature's stratagems. All those who seek spiritual liberation must worship physical union, keep it ever before their eyes, and admire and love the joys it provides: a foretaste of paradise.

Sexual and Erotic Education

*P*leasure is one of the reasons for living, and its perfect realization is one of the ways of perfecting the human being. Erotic techniques consequently were, and still are, part of the basic teaching imparted to adolescents at traditional Indian schools, including a complete theoretical knowledge of all the erotic possibilities and variations, as well as an understanding of the symbolical and magical values of sexual acts.

There are a great number of classical treatises on the erotic art, of which the most famous is the *Kama Sutra,* attributed to the sage Vatsyayana. In such treatises, the various types of men and women are classified according to their sexual aptitude and the size of their organs. They also describe the various postures possible in sexual relations. A magical significance is attributed to the various postures, and when used in erotic rituals, they correspond to Yoga postures as regards their psychophysical effect. Techniques concerning relations among persons of the same sex are illustrated too, as well as between men, women, and animals, together with all the ancillary and stimulatory elements of eroticism: hygiene, perfumes, aphrodisiacs, caresses, the subtle games of love, and so on.

The educational value of erotic sculpture is manifold. First and foremost, it attracts to the temple those who would otherwise tend to live a purely materialistic existence. Looking at the various scenes, they are unconsciously influenced by their inner, hidden meanings, of which the images are the symbols. It is essential, moreover, for anyone who has set oneself the goal of inner liberation to be free from all complexes and inhibitions. The spectacle of the love games should fill one with joy without upsetting one's

Top of a column depicting acrobatic erotics. Ramgarh, Rajputana, 10th century C.E.

detachment; they should disturb one's inner peace no more than would the sight of flowers, clouds, or birds. Contemplating love play in its most complicated and ambiguous forms is thus part of the sage's training; it is the technique of renunciation itself. This is why such images are placed above the door of the sanctuary, whose bareness evokes insensibility, the silence of nonbeing, the final goal of all existence. If a man fears that he will backslide, it is because he is only under the illusion that he has liberated himself. Erotic sights should not tempt the sage to leave the path of perfection, since there is no returning to what has truly been left behind.

posture from the Kama Sutra. Temple of Chhapri, central India, 12th century C.E.

Note on the Text and Illustrations

*T*his new edition amalgamates two texts by Alain Daniélou, *L'erotisme divinisé* (of which two limited editions were printed in 1962) and *Le temple hindou* (published in 1977), both published by Éditions Buchet/Chastel of Paris. It explains with rare clarity the complex symbolism of Hindu erotic cults and their incredibly rich iconography, which finds its maximum expression in the Hindu temple.

The illustrations are largely taken from both texts, from the Daniélou and Burnier archives, and from the collection of Jacques Cloarec, to whom our thanks are due for his kindness and ready help. The Daniélou and Burnier archives are housed by the Fondazione Cini in Venice and at the Musée de l'Elysée in Lausanne. Further information about the archives, as well as a list of the temples photographed by Raymond Burnier, is provided by the Internet site www.alaindanielou.org. On the same site, it is also possible to consult the catalogue of the library donated by Alain Daniélou through the link with Fondazione Cini.

Bibliography

Bibliographical Note by the Author
(*From the original edition of* L'erotisme divinisé)

Many literary sources refer to erotic doctrine, its symbology, and its religious and mystical meaning. These sources can be classified in various kinds, including treatises on sacred architecture; ritual manuals like the *Tantras,* in which erotic symbolism is particularly important; and lastly, books on erotic techniques.

The treatises on sacred architecture explain the necessity of erotic sculpture and summarize its role, as well as establish the arrangement of erotic images in the various parts of the temple. Major divine and human sanctions await those who build temples in which the erotic sculptures are not in the right place.

The manuals that describe the erotic rites practiced by cults and explain their philosophical, mystical, and magical meaning usually belong to a category of works known as *Tantras* or *Agamas*. There are very many such texts, and only a small number of them have ever been published. Notwithstanding the omissions deemed expedient by the publisher, the three volumes of the *Shakti Sangama Tantra* provide precious and interesting information about the symbolism of erotic postures.

Lastly, the treatises on erotic techniques define all the postures, the various kinds of relation, the temperament of the individual, and all the sizes and possible shapes of the sexual organs. These are fundamental for the sculptor, who has to consider the whole range of amorous practice. Some of these texts also serve as a philosophical and moral introduction, and provide a better understanding of the connection between erotic symbolism and the sacred character attributed to erotic practices. Relations between husband and wife, like the magical union of lovers, are considered as cosmic rites. Ceremonial acts, invocations, and magical phrases must therefore punctuate every stage.

Works Quoted or Consulted by the Author
(*In the original edition of* Le temple hindou)

In Sanskrit:

Agni Purana, Poona, 1900

Atharva Veda, Bombay, 1895–1898

Brihadaranyaka Upanishad, Madras, 1945

Brihat Shilpa Shastra (with commentary in Gujarati), Ahmedabad, 1931

Chhandogya Upanishad, Madras, 1945

Garuda Purana, Benares, 1914

Linga Purana, Bombay, 1925

Manasollasa (Someshvara), Baroda, 1925–1939

Manu Smriti, sundry editions

Shilpa Prakasha (with English translation by Alice Boner), Brill Leyden, 1966

Shilpa Shastra Manasara, Baroda, 1925

Shilpa Shastra, Lahore, 1928

Shilparatna, Trivandrum, 1929

Skanda Purana, Lucknow, 1913

Vaikhanasagama, Trivandrum, 1935

Vastuvidya, Trivandrum, 1940

Vishnu Dharmottara, Bombay, 1912

Vishvakarma prakasha (with Hindi translation), Benares, 1938

In English:

P. K. Acharya, *Indian Architecture According to Manasara Shilpa Shastra,* London, 1927